Ooops! Sometimes we make mistakes.
To find corrections to every issue of Block
go to: **www.msqc.co/corrections**

3

photo by Heidi Stock

hello
from MSQC

It's the beginning of a new year, and things are crazy here at Missouri Star! We're busy remodeling buildings and opening new stores. We have experienced so much growth in our little town this last year. We now have shops that including modern, backing, baby and kids, floral, primitives, wool, yarn, novelty, the Machine Shed and batiks. We even have a place for the non-quilters to relax while the quilters shop, dubbed "Man's Land." That may sound like a made up title, but it's actually named after an old time Hamilton men's clothing store. One of the next big projects on our plate is a remodel of the Main Shop, which includes my studio. That means I have to move too, so I'll be going back to our original building for a time. It's strange for me to go back to the beginning and as a result, I am feeling a bit nostalgic. I suppose sometimes it's good to step back and remember where the journey began. MSQC has become a much different company than I ever would have dreamed, and it is amazing to be a part of something so new and fresh! We have more ideas than time, but we are having such fun working through it. So as I sit in the room that started it all, I am overcome with gratitude for all that we have been blessed with and I am enjoying the journey!
Happy Quilting!!

Jenny

JENNY DOAN
MISSOURI STAR QUILT CO

winter is for
the birds

It's that time of year when I start to feel like this winter thing is for the birds. Cold, grey and I wish I could just fly away to some place the climate is more to my liking. Warmer days filled with sunshine, an aqua pool and a fruity drink in my hand. Ahhhhh.

Well, instead of sulking, I've decided to make the best of it and pull together some fabric. That's almost as good as a sunny day, right? Grabbing inspiration from the grey tundra outside I paired some icy neutral greys with a little pop of cheery color. I hope this puts a little sunshine into your winter days as it has mine. Happy creating!

CHRISTINE RICKS
MSQC Creative Director, BLOCK MAGAZINE

SOLIDS
FBY2423 Bella Solids - Mist
by Moda Fabrics
SKU: 9900 37

FBY12216 Bella Solids - Flax
by Moda Fabrics
SKU: 9900 241

FBY3974 Bella Solids - Silver
by Moda Fabrics
SKU: 9900 183

FBY12179 Bella Solids - Graphite
by Moda Fabrics
SKU: 9900 202

FBY12157 Bella Solids - Coral
by Moda Fabrics
SKU: 9900 147

FBY12140 Bella Solids - Washed Black
by Moda Fabrics
SKU: 9900 110

PRINTS
FBY11843 Lazy Day - Diamond Blue
by Lori Whitlock for Riley Blake
SKU: C3815-BLUE

FBY30607 Black & White - Typewriters Gray
by Cotton + Steel for Cotton+Steel
SKU: 5034-1

FBY34423 Blueberry Park - Neutral Iron Strand
by Karen Lewis for Robert Kaufman
SKU: AWI-15745-295

FBY30598 Lucky Strikes - Strikes Gray
by Kimberly Kight for Cotton+Steel
SKU: 3022-2

FBY17957 Modern Neutrals - Coral Fissure
by Amy Ellis for Moda Fabrics
SKU: 3505 14

FBY16358 Elementary - Black
by Sweetwater for Moda Fabrics
SKU: 5560 12

irish chain

quilt designed by JENNY DOAN

When I'm not quilting, you can often find me at the computer working on my other favorite hobby, family history. I have spent innumerable hours researching the Doan family tree, and I'm not the only one! There is actually a national Doan Family Association, and it has done quite a bit of investigation into the roots of our family.

It always believed that my husband's family hailed from England, but the association could never conclusively link the DNA of the American Doans to that of the English Doans. A few years ago, we decided to participate in a massive DNA test with a popular genealogy website to try to get some answers. All I had to do was ask Ron to spit in a tube, mail it off to the poor scientists who spend their days studying tubes of saliva, and wait impatiently for what would surely be mind-blowing results! When the results finally did arrive, we were thrilled to discover that the our family, while very English, is also 19 percent Irish!

For the tutorial and everything need you to make this quilt visit:
www.msqc.co/blockwinter16

It's funny how you can feel connected to a place you've never even seen. Suddenly I take personal pride in all things Irish. St. Paddy's Day is a major production, we've brushed up on all the most important superstitions, and good ol' corned beef and cabbage has made it into the menu rotation. (My husband keeps insisting I refer to him as "Ron O'Doan," but I think I'll stick to "Sweetie.")

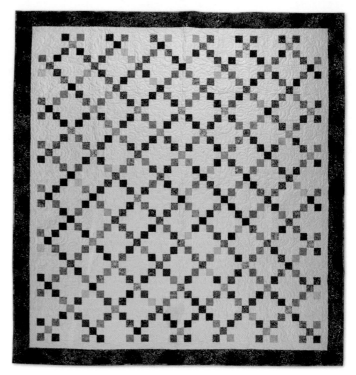

Now, of course, I have fallen in love all over again with the beautiful Irish Chain Quilt. I can't think of any other quilt pattern that is named for a country! This quilt represents an entire culture that has become near and dear to my heart, and I think it is gorgeous! The chain motif is so symbolic, too. I think of generations of Doans that connect Ron and me to our Irish ancestors as links in a chain, and the more I learn about them, the stronger that bond becomes.

As with my quilting, working on family history gives me a sense of belonging and purpose, and I feel that the accomplishments I make in my genealogical research are long-lasting and important. For me, The Irish Chain quilt represents so much of what I love: quilting and family history pieced together into one beautiful whole.

materials

makes a 91" X 97" quilt

QUILT TOP
- 1 roll of 2½" strips
- 5½ yards background – includes inner border

OUTER BORDER
- 1½ yards

BINDING
- ¾ yard

BACKING
- 8¼ yards

SAMPLE QUILT
- **Primo Batiks Radiant Reflections** by Marcus Fabrics

1 cut

From the background fabric, cut:
- (16) 6½" wide strips across the width of fabric – Subcut the strips into (91) 6½" squares.

- (24) 2½" strips across the width of the fabric.

2 make 9-patch blocks

Sew a 2½" print strip to either side of a 2½" background strip. We'll call this strip set No. 1. **Make 12** and cut (182) 2½" wide No. 1 segments. **2A**

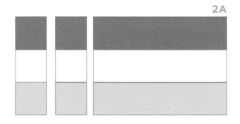

2A

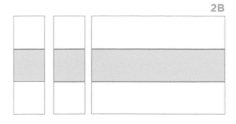

2B

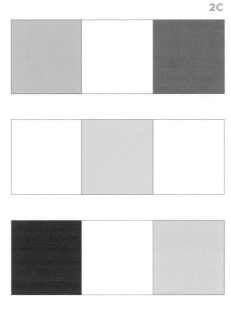

2C

Sew a 2½" background strip to either side of a 2½" print strip. We'll call this strip set 2. **Make 6** and cut (91) 2½" wide No. 2 segments. 2B

Lay out (2) No. 1 segments and (1) No. 2 segment as shown. Sew the three segments together to make (1) 9-patch block. **Make 91.** 2C

Block Size: 6" Finished.

3 arrange and sew

Lay out the blocks in **rows of 13** alternating the 6½" background squares with the 9-patch blocks. **Make 14 rows.** Rows 1, 3, 5, 7, 9, 11, and 13 begin and end with a background square. Rows 2, 4, 6, 8, 10, 12, and 14 begin and end with a 9-patch block. Once you are happy with the arrangement, sew the rows together.

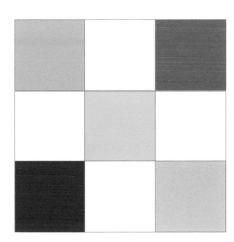

4 inner border

Cut (9) 2½" strips across the width of the background fabric. Sew the strips together end-to-end to make one long strip. Trim the border from this strip.

Refer to Borders (pg. 100) in the Construction Basics to measure and cut the inner borders. The strips are approximately 84½" for the sides and approximately 82½" for the top and bottom.

5 outer border

Cut (10) 5" strips across the width of the fabric. Sew the strips together end-to-end to make one long strip. Trim the borders from this strip.

Refer to Borders (pg. 100) in the Construction Basics to measure and cut the outer borders. The strips are approximately 88½" for the sides and approximately 91½" for the top and bottom.

6 quilt and bind

Layer the quilt with batting and backing and quilt. After the quilting is complete, square up the quilt and trim away all excess batting and backing. Add binding to complete the quilt. See Construction Basics (pg. 101) for binding instructions.

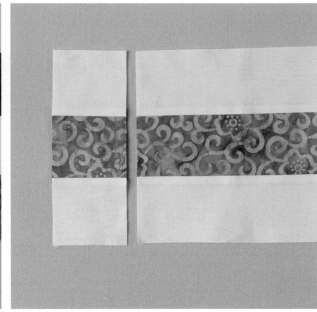

1   To make strip set 1, sew a print 2½" strip to either side of a background strip. Cut the strip set into 2½" segments. Step 2.

2   To make strip set 2, sew a background 2½" strip to either side of a print strip. Cut the strip set into 2½" segments. Step 2.

3   Lay out (2) No. 1 segments and (1) No. 2 segment and sew together to make (1) 9-patch block. Step 2.

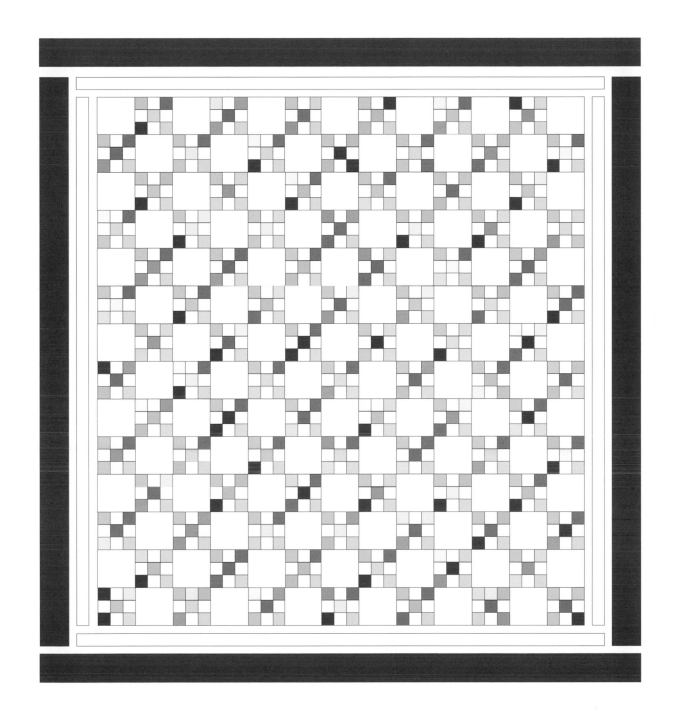

pinwheel
party

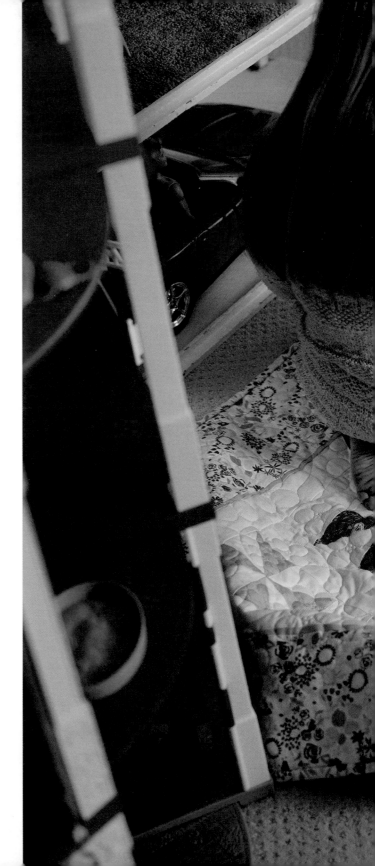

quilt designed by JENNY DOAN

When I was a small girl, my dad built a playhouse for me in the backyard. Even though the construction was simple, it was the location of countless precious memories.

Dad understood the wonders of childhood imagination, so he encouraged me to participate in the building plans. Whatever magical idea popped into my young mind, Daddy did his best to bring to life.

At my request, the little house had a Dutch door with separate pieces for the top and bottom. I loved to play inside with the bottom half closed and the top half open so I could keep an eye out for passing friends. The windows were dressed with sweet little yellow curtains that my mother and I made together. Mom wasn't much of a seamstress, but it must have been important to her that we have the experience of sewing together, and it's a memory that I will never forget!

The interior was furnished with a small red bookshelf for my play dishes, a rocking chair, a table and chair set, and a shelf that became my stove. I can't even begin to tell you how many blissful hours I spent in that playhouse. Mother helped me

For the tutorial and everything
you need to make this quilt visit:
www.msqc.co/blockwinter16

paint my simple furniture in pretty, bright colors and plant flowers all around the exterior, and I thought it was perfectly gorgeous!

I was so proud of my playhouse that I loved to invite friends over for tea parties and such. We learned a lot about getting along and working out disagreements as we played "family" and "grownups," and I got lots of practice with sharing and hosting guests. I also learned valuable lessons about the pride of ownership. It was so important to me to keep my playhouse tidy and well cared for. I had my own little broom and I think

Jenny and friends in her playhouse

JULY 1964

I must have swept that tiny, bare floor about a million times. I also diligently tended my flower garden because I knew that the outside of the house was just as important as the inside.

Looking at old pictures, I am surprised to realize just how simple my playhouse really was. It wasn't big or elaborate by any stretch of the imagination. In fact, the exterior was never even painted! But to my mind it was nothing short of a castle, and I was the princess.

materials

makes a 58½" X 63¾" quilt

QUILT TOP
- 1 package 5" print squares (42 ct.)
- 2 yards background – includes inner border
- ⅓ yard solid or contrasting color for flange

OUTER BORDER
- 1¼ yards

BINDING
- ¾ yard

BACKING
- 3¾ yards

SAMPLE QUILT
- **Aria** by Kate Spain for Moda

1 cut

From the background fabric, cut:
- (6) 5" strips across the width of the fabric – subcut into (42) 5" squares.

2 make pinwheels

Place a background square atop a print square with right sides facing. Stitch around the outer edge using a ¼" seam allowance. Cut the square from corner to corner twice on the diagonal. Each square will yield 4 half-square triangles. Open and press the seam allowance toward the darkest fabric. **2A**

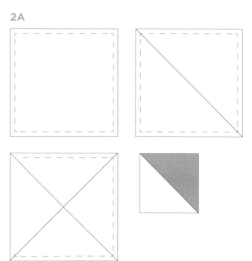

2A

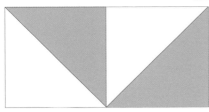

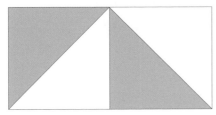

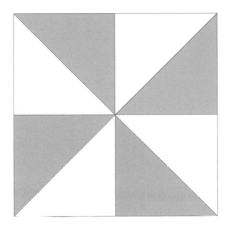

Sew 4 half-square triangles together to make a pinwheel block. **Make 42.** 2B

3 cut

From the background fabric, cut:

- (8) 2½" strips across the width of the fabric – subcut into (42) 2½" x 5¾" rectangles for vertical sashing.

4 arrange and sew

Refer to the diagram on page 23. Lay out the blocks in rows with each row consisting of **6 blocks and 6 sashing rectangles. Make 7 rows.** Rows 1, 3, 5, and 7 will all begin with a sashing rectangle and end with a pinwheel block. Rows 2, 4, and 6 will begin with a pinwheel block and end with a sashing rectangle.

Measure several rows through the center. The measurement should be approximately 44". Cut (9) 2½" strips across the width of the background fabric and sew them together end-to-end. Cut 8 strips equal to your measurement for horizontal sashing.

Sew the block rows together, adding a horizontal sashing strip between each row. Add a strip to the bottom and the top of the quilt as well.

Cut (4) 2½" background strips across the width of the fabric for the side inner border. Measure your quilt top in several places vertically (it will be approximately 53¼"). Make 2 strips to your measurement and sew one to each side of the quilt top.

5 flange and outer border

Cut (6) 1¾" strips across the width of the contrasting fabric for the flange. Sew them together end-to-end and press the strip in half. These strips need to be cut the same length as the outer border. Measure your quilt through the center vertically (approximately 53¼"). Cut 2 strips that measurement and set aside for the moment.

Cut (6) 6" wide strips across the width of the fabric from the border fabric. Sew the strips together end-to-end. Cut the outer borders from this strip.

Measure the quilt top through the center vertically (approximately 53¼"). Cut 2 strips to your measurement for the side borders. Layer the flange between the quilt top and the outer border and sew the three layers in place, one to each side of the quilt. The fold of the flange will be toward the center of the quilt.

1 Layer a print square with a background square with right sides facing. Sew all the way around the outer edge using a ¼" seam allowance. Step 2.

2 Cut the square from corner to corner twice on the diagonal. Step 2.

3 Lay out 4 half-square triangles as shown. Step 2.

4 Sew the 4 units together to complete the block. Step 2.

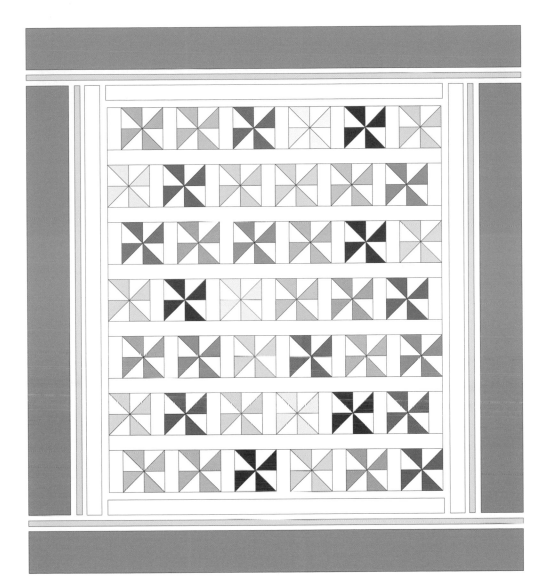

Measure the quilt top through the center horizontally (approximately 59"). Cut 2 strips from the flange fabric to your measurement. Set aside for the moment.

Cut 2 border strips to your measurement, one for the top of the quilt and one for the bottom (approximately 59"). Layer the flange between the quilt top and the outer border and sew the three layers in place. The fold of the flange will be toward the center of the quilt.

6 quilt and bind

Layer the quilt with batting and backing and quilt. After the quilting is complete, square up the quilt and trim away all excess batting and backing. Add binding to complete the quilt. See Construction Basics (pg. 101) for binding instructions.

4-patch
& snowball

quilt designed by JENNY DOAN

Years ago during our California days, we had the privilege of living in an enormous old farm house. We were able to enjoy living there paying low rent on the condition we fixed the place up. While it was a great blessing for our burgeoning family to have so much space, heating all 7,000 square feet in the winter was a bear. Our solution was to close off some of the unused rooms so we wouldn't have to heat the entire place.

For the tutorial and everything you need to make this quilt visit:
www.msqc.co/blockwinter16

Our family has a tradition of cutting down our own Christmas tree each year, and as you can imagine, we were especially excited to pick a tree for our farmhouse. The ceilings were so tall that we could cut down a much taller tree than in years past. Our chosen tree thrived in the cold living room—one of the rooms we didn't heat very often. It did so well that it lasted well through and after Christmas, still looking great. I couldn't bear to take it out, so the Christmas season continued well into the new year in the living room.

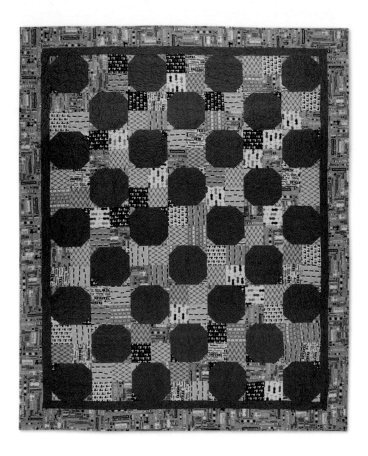

As we entered February, the tree was still going strong, so we decided to make the most of it by writing messages of love on little hearts and hanging them all over the tree. Voilà! Our very own Valentine's Day tree. Finally, after serving us so well through two holidays, we allowed the tree to enjoy its retirement and I planted it in the yard.

I suppose we were lucky to have such a cold living room. Without it, we never would have had our Valentine's tree!

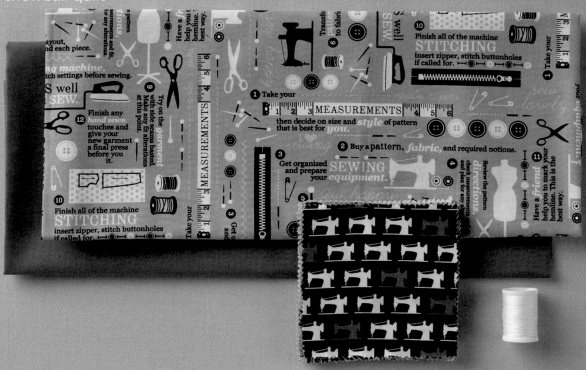

materials

makes a 77½" X 95½" quilt

QUILT TOP
- 1 package 10" squares
- 3 yards solid – includes inner border

OUTER BORDER
- 1½ yards

BINDING
- ¾ yard

BACKING
- 7¼ yards

SAMPLE QUILT
- **Sewing Studio** by Cynthia Frenette for Robert Kaufman

1 cut

From each 10" square, cut:

- (4) 5" squares

- Subcut (31) 5" squares into (4) 2½" squares for a **total of 124.**

From the solid fabric, cut:

- (8) 9½" wide strips across the width of the fabric.

- Cut the strips into (31) 9½" squares. Set aside the remainder of the fabric for the inner border.

2A

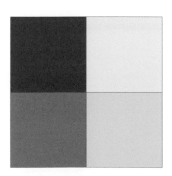

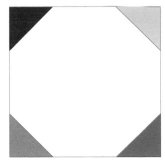

2 four-patch blocks

Make a four-patch block by sewing (4) 5″ squares together. Begin by sewing 2 squares together into a pair. Make 2 pair for each block. Press the seam allowances in opposite directions then sew the 2 pairs together. **Make 32.** 2A

3 snowball blocks

Fold (4) 2½″ squares from corner to corner once on the diagonal and press. The crease will mark your sewing line. 3A

Position a 2½″ square on one corner of a 9½″ square. Sew along the crease, trim the excess fabric away ¼″ from the sewn seam and press. Repeat for the remaining 3 corners of the square. **Make 31.** 3B

4 arrange blocks

Lay out the blocks in **9 rows** with each row consisting of **7 blocks.** Rows 1, 3, 5, 7, and 9 all begin and end with a four-patch block. Rows 2, 4, 6, and 8 all begin and end with a snowball block. Sew the rows together.

5 inner border

Cut (8) 2½″ strips across the width of the fabric. Sew the strips together end-to-end to make one long strip. Trim the borders from this strip.

Refer to Borders (pg. 101) in the Construction Basics to measure and cut the inner borders. The strips are approximately 81½″ for the sides and approximately 67½″ for the top and bottom.

6 outer border

Cut (9) 5¾″ strips across the width of the fabric. Sew the strips together end-to-end to make one long strip. Trim the borders from this strip.

Refer to Borders (pg. 100) in the Construction Basics to measure and cut the outer borders. The strips are approximately 85½″ for the sides and approximately 78″ for the top and bottom.

7 quilt and bind

Layer the quilt with batting and backing and quilt. After the quilting is complete, square up the quilt and trim away all excess batting and backing. Add binding to complete the quilt. See Construction Basics (pg. 100_ for binding instructions.

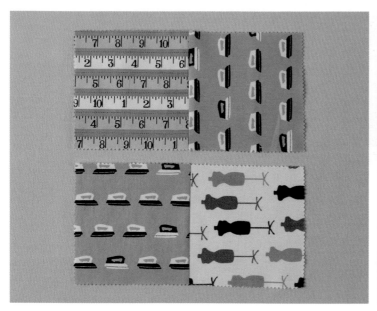

1 Sew (2) 5" squares together in pairs. Step 2.

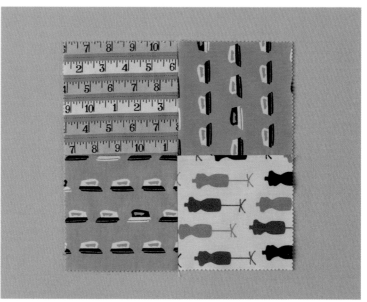

2 Sew the 2 pairs together to make (1) 4-patch block. Step 2.

3 Place a creased 2½" square on the corner of a 9½" square. Sew along the crease then trim away the excess fabric ¼" away from the sewn seam. Step 3.

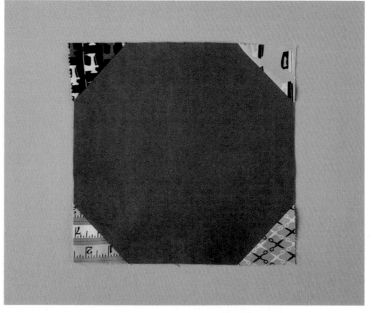

4 After all four squares have been sewn to the corners and trimmed, open the block and press. Step 3.

floating
squares

quilt designed by JENNY DOAN

We like fixing up old houses more than buying something move-in-ready. Our current house is an early-1900s Mission Victorian, and I loved it from the moment I saw it, even though it was a mess. The floor had more plaster on it than the walls—if there were walls at all! Making this house habitable involved an entire gutting and rebuilding from the floors to the plumbing. It took us two years of steady work to renovate our house, and we learned the necessary skills as we went.

However, when it came to replacing the tiles on our grand fireplace, we were dumbfounded. This wasn't any old fireplace; it was an old stand-up fireplace with a mirror on top and columns adorning it. Although we knew how to lay tile, we didn't know how to get the tile behind the fireplace. We consulted a restorationist who informed us that the fireplace wasn't actually attached to anything, and all we had to do was lay the fireplace face-down and get to work.

We insisted that the fireplace was not freestanding. It was too huge to be freestanding. But you know what? The restorationist was right! Upon arriving home, we realized the fireplace was basically floating there and all we had to do was lay it over and we could access the tile.

Just like restoring our fireplace, sometimes a quilt can seem more complicated to put together than it actually is, and this quilt is certainly an example of that!

Ron and Josh in front of the newly finished fireplace

Jenny sanding the tile

materials

makes an 45½" x 54½" quilt

QUILT TOP
- 1 package 5" squares
- 2 yards background fabric (includes border)

BINDING
- ½ yard

BACKING
- 3 yards

SAMPLE TABLE TOPPER
- **Pacific Warm** by Elizabeth Hartman for Robert Kaufman

1 cut

From the package of 5" squares, **set aside 30.**

Trim

- 5 squares to 4" – Cut the squares into (4) 2" squares.

From the background fabric, cut:

- (2) 2" strips across the WOF – Cut the strips into (40) 2" squares.

- (9) 5" strips across the WOF – Cut (49) 5" squares and (40) 2" x 5" rectangles from the strips.

To make the quilt, we need to sew squares together and make a block that has a small square in the center surrounded by background fabric.

2 floating square

To make the center of the block, sew a background 2" square to either side of a print 2" square. **2A**

Add a background 2" x 5" rectangle to either side of the center strip. **Make 20. 2B**

Sew the quilt together in rows.

Rows 1, 3, 5, 7, 9 and 11 all begin and end with a print square and alternate with a background square. **2C**

2A

2B

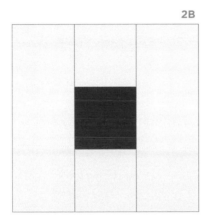

2C

2D

Rows 2, 4, 6, 8 and 10 all begin and end with a background square and alternate with a Floating Square block. **2D**

3 border

Cut (5) 3" strips across the width of the fabric. Sew the strips together end-to-end to make one long strip. Trim the borders from this strip.

Refer to Borders (pg. 100) in the Construction Basics to measure and cut the borders. The strips are approximately 50" for the sides and approximately 46" for the top and bottom.

4 quilt and bind

Layer the quilt with batting and backing and quilt. After the quilting is complete, square up the quilt and trim away all excess batting and backing. Add binding to complete the quilt. See Construction Basics (pg. 101) for binding instructions.

1 Sew a 2" background square to either side of a print square to make the center strip of the block. Step 2.

2 Lay out a background 2" x 5" rectangle on either side of a center strip. Step 2.

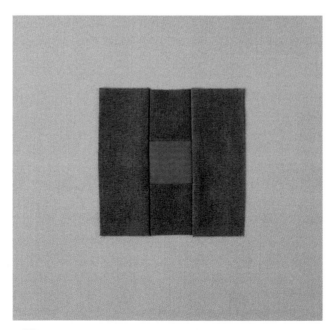

3 Sew the 3 strips together to complete the block. Step 2.

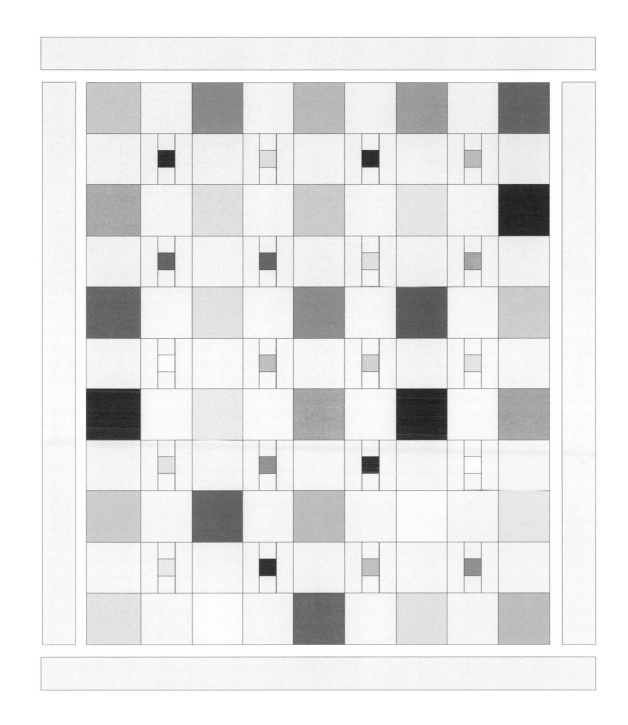

For the tutorial and everything
you need to make this quilt visit:
www.msqc.co/blockwinter16

lotus quilt

quilt designed by JENNY DOAN

Most of us love to reminisce, and more often than not, our most treasured memories come from those tender years of childhood. Life was simple, and there was a whole lot of fun to be had! It seems like everything was perfect when we were kids.

When we were kids, time ticked by more slowly. I remember a long stretch of sun-filled days from June to September when school was out and there was nothing to do but race through the neighborhood on my old pink bicycle. When you're young, it seems like months, weeks, and even days crawl by at a slow and easy pace. Now it seems like an entire year slips by so quickly I can hardly catch my breath!

When we were kids, fun was simple. I used to spend hours in the backyard constructing tiny homes for the garden fairies I hoped to one day discover. Twigs, leaves, pebbles, and berries were carefully arranged in some secret shady spot, safe from teasing brothers and snooping dogs. No wireless internet or electrical outlet needed—I had my imagination to keep me entertained!

When we were kids, life was full of magic. Christmas presents and carols; Fourth of July firework shows; the excitement of the first day of a new school year; the pure joy of easy, stress-free friendships. Happiness came easily, even on the most ordinary of days.

When we were kids, everything seemed bigger. A few years ago I had the chance to return to my childhood home, and was shocked to discover how much smaller it was than I had remembered. That basement family room that had housed movie nights and sleepovers? Tiny! How did I ever fit all my friends in such limited space? The backyard that had once been the scene of endless days of exploration and adventure? Not quite the expanse of uncharted wilderness I had believed it to be.

Jenny as a young child

Childhood is a wonderful time, but I've come to realize that we may not recall those fleeting years with perfect clarity. We tend to look back at the days of our youth with rose-colored glasses. In fact, I think our amazing little imaginations fill in the spaces to reflect experience rather than reality. It's all about perspective. Small things become large in our memory.

If you have a little one in your life, try to remember that every day, every hour, is a memory in the making. It's so easy to get caught up in the hustle and bustle of adult life. Try to slow down and see things through the eyes of a child. You'll be amazed at what you can see!

materials

makes a 67" X 76½" quilt

QUILT TOP
- 1 package (42 ct.) 10" print squares
- 1 package (42 ct.) 10" background squares

BORDER
- 1¼ yards

BINDING
- ¾ yard

BACKING
- 4¾ yards

ADDITIONAL SUPPLIES
- Large MSQC orange peel template
- 7¼ yards Heat N Bond Feather Lite Fusible Interfacing

SAMPLE QUILT
- **Into the Deep** by Patty Sloniger for Michael Miller

1 cut

Place the large orange peel template atop each print square (the template will reach from corner to corner on the diagonal) and cut around the template. **Cut 42.** 1A

Place the template atop the interfacing and cut **42 pieces.** The interfacing is so lightweight that you can cut multiple layers at one time. Just fan fold the interfacing back and forth before you place your template. 1B

Notice that one side of the interfacing feels bumpy. The bumpy side is the side that is fusible.

1A

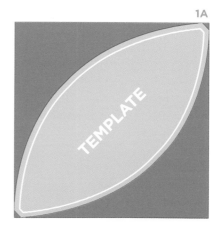

TEMPLATE

1B

interfacing

1C

cut line

cut along
interfacing side

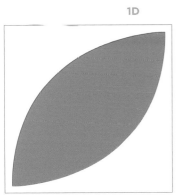

1D

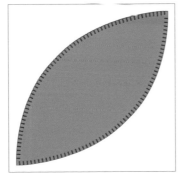

1E

Before you layer the interfacing and the fabric piece together, cut a slit in the interfacing. Then place the bumpy side of the interfacing toward the right side of a print orange peel piece. Stitch all the way around the outer edge of the layered pieces using a ¼" seam allowance. 1C

Gently turn the orange peel right side out. Smooth out the edges so the piece lies flat. Place the peel on the background square on the diagonal with the bumpy side facing the right side of the square and press in place.

Note: the piece will be about ¼" from each corner. 1D

Stitch the orange peel in place using a small blanket stitch or, if you choose, a pretty decorative stitch. **Make 42 blocks.** 1E

Block Size: 9½" Finished

2 arrange

We arranged our blocks in a chevron pattern with **6 blocks** across and **7 blocks** down. Feel free to play with the layout because this design can be easily changed just by turning some of the blocks.

Once you are happy with the layout, sew the blocks together into rows. Press the seam allowances of the odd numbered rows toward the right and the even numbered rows toward the left. This will make the seams nest.

3 border

Cut (8) 5½" strips across the width of the fabric. Sew the strips together end-to-end to make one long strip. Trim the borders from this strip.

Refer to Borders (pg. 100) in the Construction Basics to measure and cut the borders. The strips are approximately 67" for the sides and approximately 67½" for the top and bottom.

4 quilt and bind

Layer the quilt with batting and backing and quilt. After the quilting is complete, square up the quilt and trim away all excess batting and backing. Add binding to complete the quilt. See Construction Basics (pg. 101) for binding instructions.

1 Place the large orange peel template atop each print square and cut around the template. Step 1.

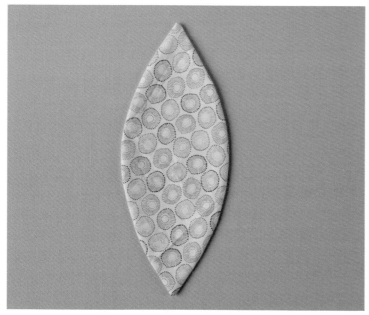

2 Turn the orange peel right side out. Step 1.

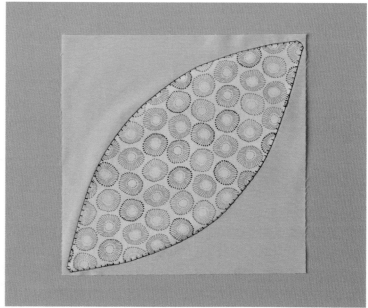

3 Applique the orange peel in place using a small blanket stitch. Step 1.

47

For the tutorial and everything you need to make this quilt visit:
www.msqc.co/blockwinter16

double
square star

quilt designed by JENNY DOAN

As a mother of seven, I'm sure glad I adore children. Yes, with kids come messes, chaos, and a whole lot of noise, but there are few things as wonderful as watching the simple joys of childhood from a parental perspective! Children are so fabulously easy to entertain. They find fun and adventure everywhere they go, and don't require piles of money or extravagant plans to create a memorable experience. All you need is time, a little patience, and the freedom to explore. And the littler they are, the easier they are to impress! (Teenagers, however, are another story.)

When our kids were small, we loved to feed the ducks at our favorite local park. All throughout the week, we saved the heels of the bread that no one wanted to eat, and when we had a good bagful, we'd fix a picnic, pile into the car, and head off for an afternoon of fun.

49

Jenny and kids feeding the ducks at the pond.

Amid a flurry of giggles and jelly-stained smiles, we'd soon notice a small gang of ducks inching closer to our feast. Pretty soon one of the kids would throw a piece of sandwich to the birds, which only served to embolden those cheeky little duckies, and they'd venture closer and closer, begging for another taste.

Though I'd scold the kids for feeding the ducks with their sandwiches instead of the bread heels, my attempt at parenting made little difference. The moment that first morsel of sandwich hit the ground, the ducks lost all fear, and we were under attack! Squeals of delight from the children mingled with frantic quacks as our picnic devolved into a cloud of feathers and breadcrumbs.

The kids would race around, each with their own crew of ducks trailing close behind. We tossed handfuls of bread pieces to our hungry pursuers until every last crumb was gone. Even then, there were always a few stragglers that stayed close by "just in case." What fun we had picnicking with those ducks!

It's just amazing that with a basketful of sandwiches and a picnic quilt we had all that was necessary for an afternoon of pure delight for our little family. How I miss those easy times!

materials

makes a 62" X 75" quilt

QUILT TOP
- 3 packages 5" squares of the same fabric line
- 1¾ yards background

OUTER BORDER
- 1¼ yards

BINDING
- ¾ yard

BACKING
- 4 yards

SAMPLE PROJECT
- **Botanique** by Lila Tueller for Riley Blake

1 sort

Sort the 5" squares so there are 3 squares of the same color/print together. You will need 40 groups of 3 squares.

2 cut

From each group of 3 squares, cut (1) 5" square into 2½" squares. You'll have a total of (160) 2½" squares and (80) 5" squares. Keep all of the same color/prints together.

From the background fabric, cut:

- (80) 2½" x 5" rectangles
- (80) 2½" x 7" rectangles

3 sew

Select (1) 5" square and (2) matching 2½" squares. Fold a matching 2½" square from corner to corner once on the diagonal. Press the crease in place to mark your sewing line. Sew a square to the right end of a 2½" x 5" rectangle as shown using the crease as your sewing line. Trim the excess fabric ¼" away from your sewing line. Open and press the seam allowance toward the darker fabric. **3A**

Fold the other matching square from corner to corner once on the diagonal and press the crease in place to mark your sewing line.

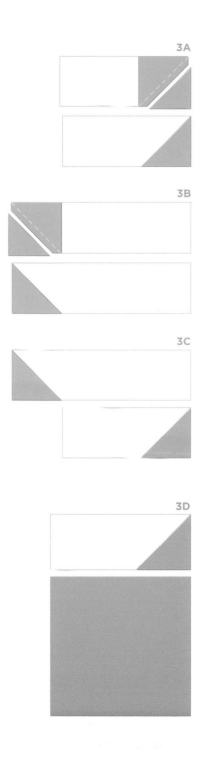

3A

3B

3C

3D

3E

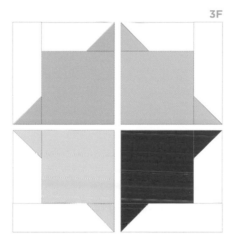

3F

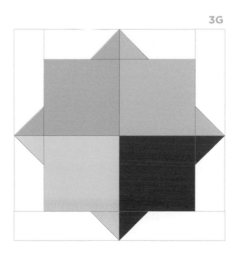

3G

Sew the 2½" square to the left end of (1) 2½" x 7" rectangle as shown. Trim the excess fabric ¼" away from your sewing line. Open and press the seam allowance toward the darker fabric. 3B

Notice that the short rectangle and the longer rectangle have the squares sewn to opposing ends and are mirror images of each other. 3C

Stitch the shorter rectangle to the 5" square. 3D

Sew the longer rectangle to the square as shown. 3E

This makes up one quadrant of the block. **Make 4**. 3F

Sew the 4 quadrants together to complete the block. **Make 20**. 3G

Block Size: 13" Finished

Sew the blocks together into **rows of 4. Make 5 rows.**

Arrange the rows to your satisfaction. Press the even numbered rows toward the right and the odd numbered rows toward the left. This will make the seams nest.

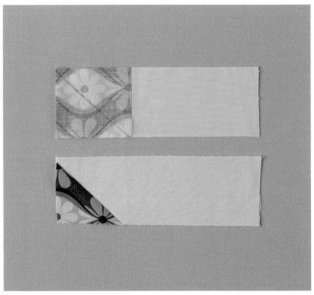

1 Sew a 2½"square on the diagonal to the right end of a 2½" x 5" rectangle. Trim the excess fabric ¼" away from the sewn seam, open and press. Step 3.

2 Sew a 2½" square on the diagonal to the left end of a 7" rectangle. Trim ¼" away from the sewn seam, open and press. Step 3.

3 Sew the shorter strip to the top of the block and the longer strip to the side of the block. Step 3.

4 Sew 4 quadrants together to complete the block. Step 3.

4 borders

From the border fabric, cut: (7) 5½"
strips across the width of the fabric. Sew
the strips end-to-end to make one long
strip. Sew the strips together. Trim the
borders from this strip.

Refer to Borders (pg. 100) in the
Construction Basics to measure and cut
the borders. The strips are approximately
65½" for the sides and approximately
62½" for the top and bottom.

5 quilt and bind

Layer the quilt with batting and backing
and quilt. After the quilting is complete,
square up the quilt and trim away all
excess batting and backing. Add binding
to complete the quilt. See Construction
Basics (pg. 101) for binding instructions.

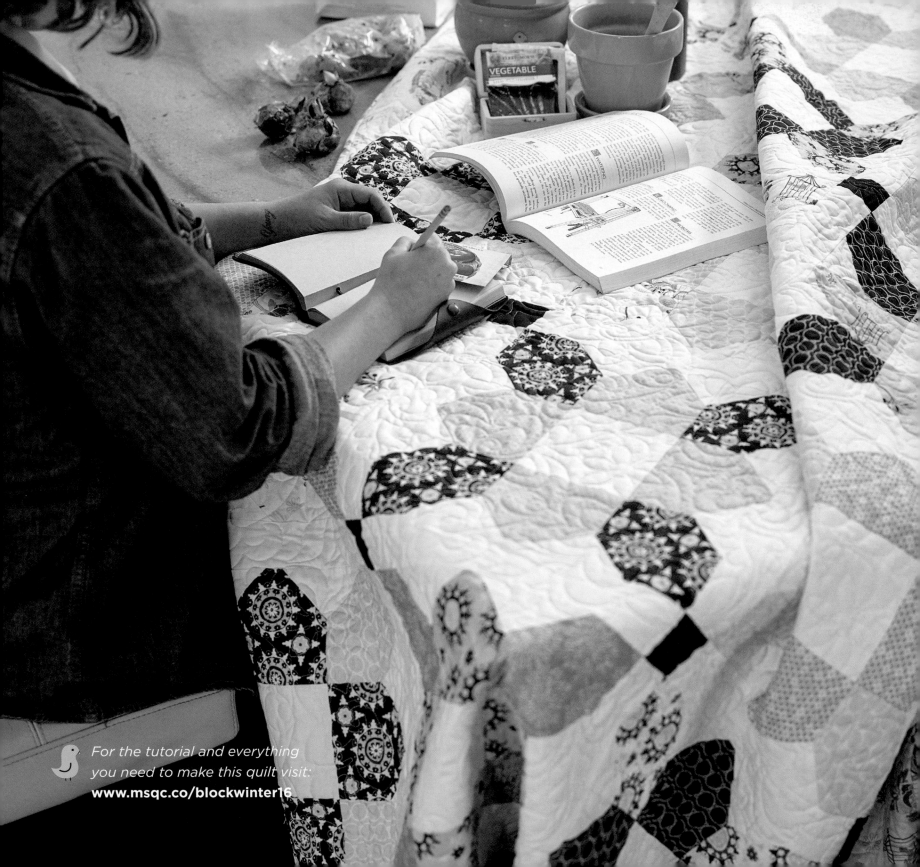

For the tutorial and everything
you need to make this quilt visit:
www.msqc.co/blockwinter16

prairie
flowers

quilt designed by JENNY DOAN

This might sound a little funny, but I love to get my hands covered in rich garden soil, and there are few things as relaxing as sitting in the quiet of the yard, working through an arsenal of weeds until the sun goes down. I get to work out a little aggression, and the yard is left looking as neat and tidy as a magazine cover! It's almost as good as therapy! Best of all, it's so rewarding to see the yard burst into a rainbow of blooms and to be able to feed the family from the garden throughout the summer. (Who's going to complain about another night of BLTs? No one, that's who!).

I started gardening with my kids when they were very small. Children and gardens are a match made in heaven. Digging in the dirt, discovering an array of worms and bugs, and operating the watering can are only the beginning of the fun! The real magic comes when the plants start to grow and the children get to see the fruits of their labor. After all, there's no better way to teach children the law of the harvest than to let them experience it for themselves. A tummy full of juicy strawberries, tomatoes, and corn on the cob has a powerful way of imprinting in a child's heart that you reap what you sow. In other words, if you want jack-o'-lanterns at Halloween, you better get your hiney off that computer and come help with the weeding, young man!

When my daughter Sarah was young, she often carried a little yellow watering can all over the yard as I planted. The moment I got a flower in the ground, Sarah was there to give it a good drink of water. She took this responsibility very seriously. Even on rainy days Sarah would wake up in the morning determined to head out to water her flowers.

As the kids grew older, proactiveness took a back seat to other interests, and it became necessary to make assignments to help out in the yard. I remember one summer when we had been particularly busy and the garden was suffering from neglect. Weeds permeated throughout our once—vibrant Eden, and I worried that the season might be a lost cause. I gathered the whole gang and announced that it was time for a "family night." Grabbing a spool of twine, I marked the garden off into nine equal parts, putting each family member in charge of a section.

With the promise of hot fudge sundaes for those who cleared their patches, we got to work and, wouldn't you know it, at the end of the night our garden looked as healthy and neat as ever, and we laughed and joked as we enjoyed our sweet rewards.

Good things come not to those who just sit around and wait, but to those who are willing to get their hands a little dirty! I'm grateful for those important lessons I was able to share with my children in the garden!

materials

makes a 74" x 89½" quilt

QUILT TOP
- 1 package 10" squares
- 3½ yards background fabric (includes sashing and inner border)
- ¼ yard for cornerstones

OUTER BORDER
- 1½ yards

BINDING
- ¾ yard

BACKING
- 5½ yards

SAMPLE QUILT
- **Lulabelle** by Dodi Lee Poulsen for Riley Blake

1 cut

From each 10" square, cut:

- (4) 5" squares for a **total of 160** squares.

From the background fabric, cut:

- (20) 2½" strips across the width of fabric. Subcut the strips into 2½" squares for a **total of 320**.

- (3) 5" strips across the width of the fabric. Subcut the strips into 5" squares for a **total of 20.**

- (11) 2½" strips across the width of the fabric. Subcut the strips into (31) 14" x 2½" rectangles for sashing.

From the cornerstone fabric, cut:

- (1) 2½" strip across the width of fabric. Subcut the strip into 2½" squares for a **total of 12**.

2 block construction

Fold a 2½" square from corner to corner on the diagonal and press the crease in place. The crease marks your sewing line. Prepare (16) 2½" squares. **2A**

Sew a 2½" square onto 2 opposing corners of a 5" square. Trim each ¼" away from the seam line. These units go on the corners of the block. **Make 4** and set aside for the moment. **2B**

2A

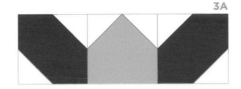

3A

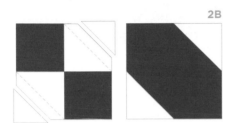

2B

3B

2C

3C

Sew (2) 2½" squares to 2 corners of a 5" square as shown. The squares are on adjacent corners. These units go between the corner units. **Make 4.** 2C

3 sew rows

Sew a corner unit to either side of a center unit as shown. **Make 2 rows** like this. 3A

Sew a center unit to either side of a 5" square. **Make 1 row** like this. 3B

Sew the three rows together to make one block. 3C
Make 20 blocks.

Block Size: 13½" Finished

4 arrange and sew

Lay out the blocks in rows, with each row containing **4 blocks.** Once you are happy with the appearance, sew the blocks together into rows adding a 2½" x 14" sashing rectangle between each. **Make 5 rows** and press the odd numbered rows toward the left and the even numbered rows toward the right.

4A

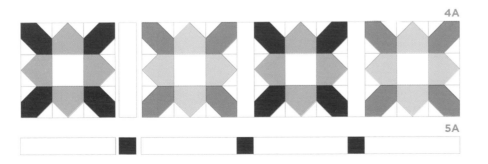

4A

5A

5 sashing strip

Sew a 2½" square (cornerstone) to a 2½" x 14" sashing rectangle. Add a 2½" square, then another sashing rectangle. Continue on in this manner until you have sewn a strip containing

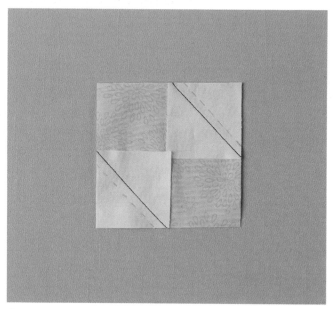

1 Place a 2½″ square on two opposing corners of a 5″ square. Sew along the diagonal of the small square from corner to corner. Trim the excess fabric ¼″ away from the sewn seam. Step 2.

2 After the unit has been trimmed, open and press. Step 2.

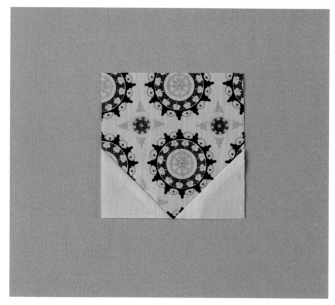

3 Sew a 2½″ square on the diagonal of the 2 corners that are adjacent on a 5″ print square. Trim the excess fabric away ¼″ from the seam allowance, open and press. Step 2.

4 Arrange the units into 3 rows as shown and sew the rows together to complete the block. Step 3.

3 cornerstones and 4 sashing rectangles. Make 4 sashing strips. 5A

Sew a sashing strip between each row of blocks.

6 inner border

Cut (8) 2½" strips across the width of the fabric. Sew the strips together end-to-end to make one long strip. Trim the borders from this strip.

Refer to Borders (pg. 100) in the Construction Basics to measure and cut the inner borders. The strips are approximately 76" for the sides and approximately 64½" for the top and bottom.

7 outer border

Cut (8) 5½" strips across the width of the fabric. Sew the strips together end-to-end to make one long strip. Trim the borders from this strip.

Refer to Borders (pg. 100) in the Construction Basics to measure and cut the outer borders. The strips are approximately 80" for the sides and approximately 74½" for the top and bottom.

8 quilt and bind

Layer the quilt with batting and backing and quilt. After the quilting is complete, square up the quilt and trim away all excess batting and backing. Add binding to complete the quilt. See Construction Basics (pg. 101) for binding instructions.

For the tutorial and everything
you need to make this quilt visit:
www.msqc.co/blockwinter16

studio
star

quilt designed by JENNY DOAN

One of the best parts of my job is getting to attend Quilt Market every year. Designers, vendors, and quilters from all over the world gather together under one gigantic roof in an explosion of color, pattern, and innovation. In other words, it's a quilter's paradise!

It is overwhelming to walk down aisle after aisle and soak up all the creativity on display. Quilts, fabric, and notions take up the majority of the space, but every once in awhile we happen upon something unique. One year as I was exploring the convention hall, I discovered a display of decorative metal "quilt blocks." There were countless different patterns,

and they were so cute, I just had to have some! We bought a whole collection of blocks to decorate the quilt shops in Hamilton. (And, of course, we had to make a large order of the Missouri Star block to sell!) As I looked over the display, I took a liking to one particular block. Though I didn't know the name of the pattern, it was so pretty that I took it home and hung it on the back door of my studio.

Fast forward a few years and I was sitting in my studio trying to come up with an idea for a new set of YouTube tutorials. My studio is situated such that when I sit at my desk, I face the back door. I have literally stared at that metal block day after day for years! So as our team chatted about possible quilt patterns, my eyes once again wandered up to that block, and it dawned on me: We needed to do my mystery block!

I did a little research and discovered that, like many old blocks, this block has several different names including "Sister's Choice" and "Father's Choice." I decided to give our version a new name based on its longtime home on my studio door: The Studio Star!

So I worked to come up with a quick, easy way to construct this classic block using our favorite secret weapon: precuts! And just like that, a star was born... The Studio Star!

materials

makes a 62" X 82" quilt

QUILT TOP
- 1 roll 2½" print strips
- 3¼ yards background fabric – includes inner border

OUTER BORDER
- 1 yard

BINDING
- ¾ yard

BACKING
- 5 yards

SAMPLE QUILT
- **Black Tie Affair** by BasicGrey for Moda

1 cut

Note: We will be cutting out two blocks at a time!

Select 2 contrasting print strips. Layer the two strips together and cut:

- (1) 2½" square (you're cutting through **2 layers** so 1 cut will yield **2 squares**.)

- (4) 4½" rectangles (again, you're cutting through **2 layers** so you will have a total of **8 rectangles**.)

From the background fabric, cut:

- (36) 2½" strips across the width of the fabric.

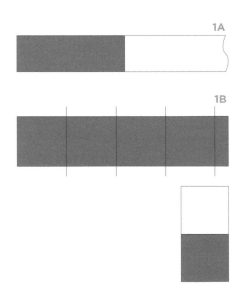

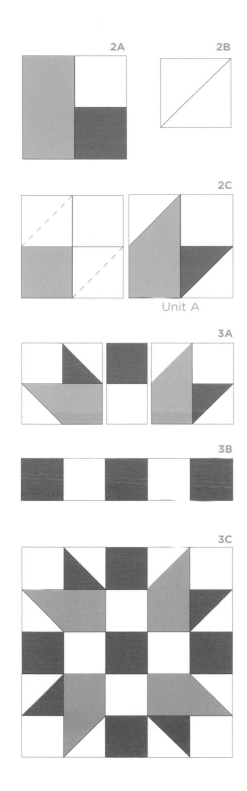

2A

2B

2C

Unit A

3A

3B

3C

Set aside the (1) 2½" square of one print and the (4) 4½" rectangles of the other. These will be used to make the second block.

Stitch a background strip to the remainder of each print strip. The background fabric will extend beyond the print strip. Trim the background strips even with the print. From the remainder of the background strips, cut (8) 2½" squares for a **total of 16. Set aside 8** for the second block. **1A**

Layer the two sewn strip sets, one atop the other, and cut (8) 2½" pieces. This will give you **(16) 2-patch units**, 8 of each color. Set aside **(8) 2-patch** units that have the same print as the 2½" square for the second block. **1B**

2 block construction

Press the (8) 2-patch units open.

Sew a 2½" x 4½" rectangle to a 2-patch unit. Sew the two together using a ¼" seam allowance.
Make 4 units. 2A

Fold the (8) 2½" background squares once on the diagonal. Press the crease in place to use as your sewing line. **2B**

Place a creased background square on 2 corners of the unit and sew each in place on the diagonal. Then trim the excess fabric away ¼" from the seam line, open and press. **Make 4** of these corner units, we'll call them **Unit A** for clarity. **2C**

3 lay out the units

Lay out the block in rows. Rows 1 and 3 are made by placing a Unit A on either side of a 2-patch unit. Be aware of the direction the corners are placed. **3A**

Row 2 is made by sewing a 2-patch unit to either side of a 2½" square. **3B**

Sew the three rows together to complete one block. **3C**

Pick up the pieces you set aside when cutting to make another block. **Make 35 blocks.**

4 arrange blocks

Sew the blocks together into **rows of 5. Make 7 rows.** Press the seam allowances of the odd numbered rows toward the left and the even rows toward the right. That will make the seams nest and it will be easier to make the corners match.

5 inner border

Cut (7) 2½" strips across the width of the fabric. Sew the strips together end-to-end to make one long strip. Trim the borders from this strip.

Cut (4) 2½" squares from one of the remaining print strips. Set aside for the inner cornerstones.

Measure the quilt top in three different places vertically. Stay away from the edges while measuring. Cut two strips to your measurement (approximately 70½" for each side. Sew a strip to either side of the quilt.

Measure the quilt top in three different places horizontally. Again, stay away from the edges. Cut two strips to your measurement (approximately 50½"). Sew a print cornerstone to either end of each of the strips. Sew one strip to the top of the quilt and the other to the bottom.

1   Press the 2½" two-patch units open. Step 2.

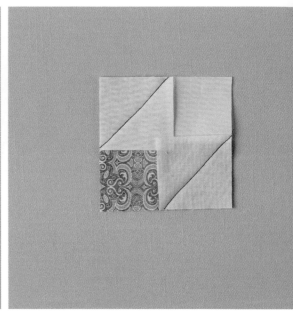

2   Sew a 2½" x 4½" rectangle together. Step 2.

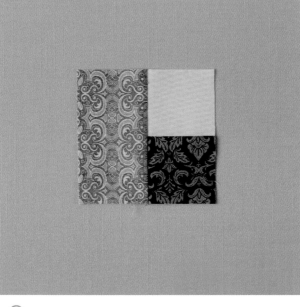

3   Place a 2½" background square on two opposing corners of the unit. Sew on the diagonal, trim ¼" away from the sewn seam. Step 2.

4   Open the unit and press. Step 2.

5   Make the top and bottom rows of the block by sewing a corner unit to either side of a 2-patch unit. Step 2.

6   Make the center row by sewing a 2-patch unit to either side of a 2½" square. Step 2.

6 outer border

Cut (8) 4½" strips across the width of the fabric. Sew the strips together end-to-end to make one long strip. Trim the borders from this strip.

Cut (4) 4½" rectangles from one of the remaining strips and (4) 2½" squares from a contrasting strip. Refer to the directions for making Unit A under Block Construction. **Make 4** to use as cornerstones in the outer border. Set aside for the moment.

Measure the quilt top in three different places vertically. Stay away from the edges while measuring. Cut two strips to your measurement (approximately 74½" for each side. Sew a strip to either side of the quilt.

Measure the quilt top in three different places horizontally. Again, stay away from the edges. Cut two strips to your measurement (approximately 54½"). Sew a Unit A cornerstone to either end of each of the strips. Sew one strip to the top of the quilt and the other to the bottom.

7 quilt and bind

Layer the quilt with batting and backing and quilt. After the quilting is complete, square up the quilt and trim away all excess batting and backing. Add binding to complete the quilt. See Construction Basics (pg. 101) for binding instructions.

For the tutorial and everything
you need to make this quilt visit:
www.msqc.co/blockwinter16

new
flying
geese

quilt designed by JENNY DOAN

People often ask me how on earth I come up with a new quilt pattern every single week. I suppose there are only so many ways to put together squares and triangles, but we haven't run out yet! The key is adding an element of surprise, something special that lends a unique touch to an old favorite block.

In quilting, as in life, it's always fun to wander away from the old familiar path to see what lies beyond. I really do love the unexpected. This quilt is a Flying Geese, which is one of the most common blocks in quilting, but this version is different because it is dimensional. The sides of each flying geese triangle are open, like pockets. This simple little touch makes the design of this quilt stand out from the ordinary.

One year as our anniversary drew near, I was scrambling to come up with something special for Ron. It had been a rough year, and I so wanted to surprise him with something more than just dinner and a movie. Life had put us through the wringer, and we needed some time together.

Ron loves motorcycles and racing, so I quietly borrowed (see: stole) one of his motorcycle magazines and searched for inspiration. Though I didn't exactly know what I was doing, I found an ad for a race I thought Ron would enjoy and bought tickets. All I knew was it was some sort of package, and anything with speeding bikes would make my husband happy, so I wrapped up my gift and presented it with a kiss.

As luck would have it, our tickets turned out to be for the Supercross, the biggest race of the year! Ron was elated, and as we found our seats, he thought he'd died and gone to heaven! We were positioned front and center, right in front of the action! In buying the tickets, I had only been thinking of Ron and what he would enjoy, but I was surprised to discover that I was having a wonderful time as well.

Our favorite part of the event was also the most unexpected. During intermission, Brock Glover, one of the top racers of his day, came out onto the track sporting hot pink leathers from head to foot - quite a change from typical racing attire. The surprised crowd was up on its feet cheering and howling, and when I looked over at Ron I saw that sparkle in his eyes that I have come to love so

much. Perhaps it wasn't the most romantic of anniversaries, but it was certainly uniquely fabulous!

Over the years Ron and I have had many interesting adventures together, and I wouldn't trade any one of them for a more traditional, ordinary romance. Who needs ordinary when extraordinary is on the horizon? Don't be afraid to try something new. Quilts and romance alike are only made more exciting with a little variety (and hot pink leathers) to spice things up!

“ When I looked over at Ron I saw that sparkle in his eyes that I have come to love so much. Perhaps it wasn't the most romantic of anniversaries, but it was certainly uniquely fabulous! ”

materials

makes a 54" X 63" quilt

QUILT TOP
- 1 package (42 ct.) 10" squares
- 4 packages (42 ct.) white 5" squares background *or* 3 yards cut into 5" squares

BINDING
- ½ yard

BACKING
- 3½ yards

SAMPLE QUILT
- **Sunprints** by Allison Glass for Andover

1 cut and fold

Cut each 10" square in half once, making a 5" x 10" rectangle.

Fold the rectangles in half with wrong sides together.

Layer a 5" white square, right side up, with a folded rectangle. Position the rectangle about ½" down from the top of the white square. Then place a white square on top of the two pieces. Align the tops of the two white squares. The top square should be facing down. **1A**

1A

2A

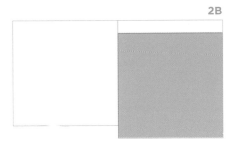

2B

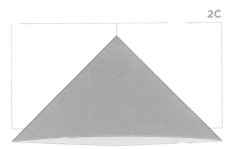

2C

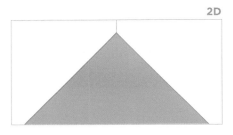

2D

2 sew

Stitch down one side of the layered pieces. 2A

Press the seam allowance to set it, then open the top square and press the rectangle toward one side of the unit. 2B

Lift and bring down the center of the fold of the rectangle to match the seam allowance.
Note: The fold of the rectangle will lay right on top of the seam line, thus creating a 3-dimensional flying geese block. 2C

Press and trim the bottom of the rectangle to match the bottom of the white squares. The block should measure 5″ x 9½″ unfinished after trimming. **Make 84** 2D

Block Size: 4½″ x 9″ finished

3 arrange and sew

Sew the Flying Geese into **rows of 6**. **Make 14 rows** and sew the rows together.

4 quilt and bind

Layer the quilt with batting and backing and quilt. After the quilting is complete, square up the quilt and trim away all excess batting and backing. Add binding to complete the quilt. See Construction Basics (pg. 101) for binding instructions.

1 Stitch down one side of the layered squares. Step 2.

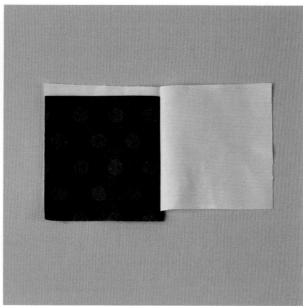

2 Open the top square and press the rectangle toward one side. Step 2.

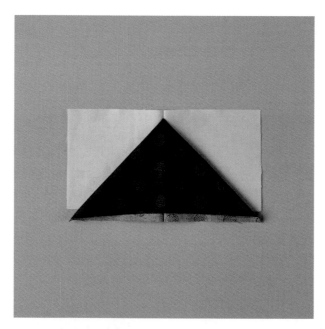

3 Lift and bring down the center of the fold of the rectangle so it matches the seam allowance of the two sewn squares. Trim so the bottom edges are even. Step 2.

For the tutorial and everything you need to make this quilt visit:
www.msqc.co/blockwinter16

ribbon
star

quilt designed by JENNY DOAN

Years ago when our family was young, I gave my husband a plaque that read, "Any man can be a father, but it takes someone special to be a daddy." Ron took to fatherhood like a duck to water! He loved our little ones unconditionally and without reservation. And best of all, he always took the time to play with them!

Ron was a mechanic and a motorcycle racer in his younger years, and even though he left that high-octane life behind by the time we had children, he still used his motorcycle as his primary mode of transportation. Every day as it came time for him to arrive home from work, the kids would start looking out the window for Daddy. And the moment they heard the roar of his motorcycle, they'd tear out the front door, run to greet him, and start begging for a ride.

Luckily, Ron was just as happy to see the kids as they were to see him, and he'd scoop them up into his arms while situating them carefully around him on the bike. As they slowly rode

Ron and the kids on the motorcycle

around our circle drive, giggles and squeals of delight echoed just about as loudly as the motorcycle engine itself!

When I look at this old photo, I am taken back to those days when nothing mattered as much as Daddy's homecoming. I absolutely love that Sarah is wearing pearls and cowboy boots, as if she had been interrupted in the middle of a very important session of playing dress-up. It never mattered what they were doing or what they were wearing, when Ron came around the corner, the kids were there waiting.

"Any man can be a father, but it takes someone special to be a daddy."

I've known dads who, at the end of a long day at work, are more interested in relaxing in the recliner or unwinding with a hot shower than in wrestling and playing with a whole passel of eager children. Not Ron. When it comes to the children, Ron has always had an endless supply of patience and energy. I truly could not have asked for a better companion in parenthood!

materials
makes a 68" X 82" quilt

QUILT TOP
- 1 roll of 2½" print strips
- 1 roll of 2½" white strips (42 ct.) *or* 3 yards background fabric

OUTER BORDER
- 1½ yards

BINDING
- ¾ yard

BACKING
- 5 yards

SAMPLE QUILT
- **Dreamweaver** by Amy Butler for Free Spirit

1 cut
Select (20) 2½" x 42" print strips. From each, cut:

- (4) 2½" x 6½" rectangles. Keep each set of four together.

Select (20) 2½" x 42" print strips. From each, cut:

- (4) 2½" x 4½" rectangles. Keep each set of four together.

From the leftover pieces of the 2½" print strips, select 20. From each, cut:

- (4) 2½" squares. Keep each set of four together.

From the remaining pieces of the 2½" print strips, cut:

- (30) 2½" squares for sashing cornerstones. Set aside.

From the background fabric, cut:

- (240) 2½" squares
- (80) 2½" x 4½" rectangles
- (49) 2½" x 12½" rectangles – Set aside for sashing

84

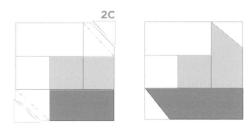

2A

2B

2C

2D

2 make a corner unit

Sew a 2½" background square to a 2½" print square. Add a 2½" x 4½" background strip as shown. **2A**

Sew a print 4½" strip to one side of the unit as shown. Add a print 6½" strip to the adjacent side. **2B**

Fold 2 background 2½" squares from corner to corner once on the diagonal and press the crease in place. Using the crease as your sewing line, stitch a square to each of the two print strips of the unit as shown. Trim the excess fabric ¼" away from the seam line. **Make 4** for each block. **2C**

Sew the 4 corner units together to complete the block. **Make 20 blocks. 2D**

3 arrange and sew

Lay out the blocks in rows, with each row containing **4 blocks**. Once you are happy with the appearance, sew the blocks together into rows adding a 2½" x 12½" sashing rectangle between each block and on the two outside edges. **Make 5 rows. 3A**

4 sashing strips

Sew a 2½" square (cornerstone) to a 2½" x 12½" sashing rectangle. Add a 2½" square, then another sashing rectangle. Continue on in this manner until you have sewn a strip containing 5 cornerstones and 4 sashing rectangles. **Make 6 sashing strips. 4A**

Sew a sashing strip between each row of blocks. Finish the center of the quilt by sewing one sashing strip to the top of the quilt and one to the bottom.

5 border

From the border fabric, cut:

- (7) 5½" strips across the width of the fabric.

Sew the strips end-to-end to make one long strip. Sew the strips together. Trim the borders from this strip.

Refer to Borders (pg. 100) in the Construction Basics to measure and cut the inner borders. The strips are approximately 72½" for the sides and approximately 68½" for the top and bottom.

6 quilt and bind

Layer the quilt with batting and backing and quilt. After the quilting is complete, square up the quilt and trim away all excess batting and backing. Add binding to complete the quilt. See Construction Basics (pg. 101) for binding instructions.

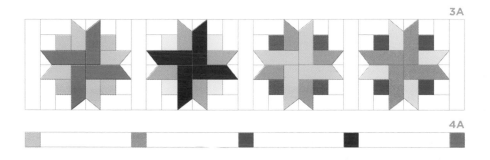

3A

4A

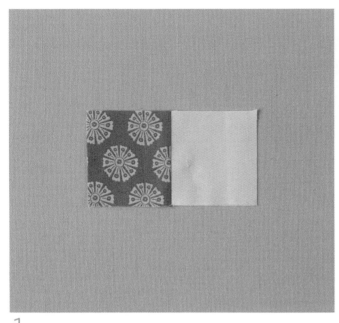

1 Sew a print 2½″ square to a background 2½″ square. Step 2.

2 Sew a 2½″ x 4½″ background strip to the 2-patch unit. Step 2.

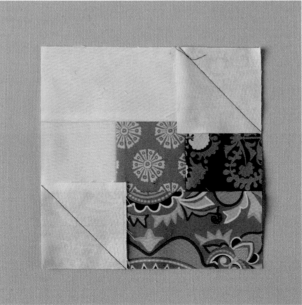

3 Add a print 2½″ x 4½″ strip to one side of the unit and a print 2½″ x 6½″ strip to the adjacent side. Step 2.

4 Place a 2½″ background square on two corners of the unit as shown. Sew on the diagonal, trim ¼″ away from the sewn seam, open and press. Step 2.

5 Sew 4 quadrants together to complete the block. Step 2.

MSQC is growing

What a great adventure we're on. I can hardly believe we're getting ready to start our third year of Block magazine. So many wonderful things have happened this past year and we look forward to the coming year with excitement. We have a huge main shop remodel planned, and lots of fun events to keep us all busy and entertained.

The Modern shop is a place for modern designers to come together. We have special displays that feature individual designers, giving a little bit of information about them, their inspiration, and their fabric. Come on in and find your favorite designers. But beware, you may just fall in love with a few new designers as well.

The Machine Shed is your one stop shop for notions. In this store you can find thread, rotary cutters, scissors, templates, rulers, tape measures, buttons, the list goes on and on. We even have a full line of Baby Lock Sewing machines available to test drive and enjoy.

Mans Land is a place for quilters and non quilters to take a rest from a busy day of shopping. Its named after an old Hamilton

Iron to the dark side!

(whenever possible!)

IT'S ABOUT COMPLETION,

NOT PERFECTION.

Some quilts are born from

an idea for a pattern;

others are inspired by the fabrics

Mens Clothing Store that we just loved. We've tried to create a cozy space for folks to come together and rest for a bit. Feel free to relax in an easy chair, read a little, watch a little TV, play a game of pool, or chat with some new found friends.

Mama Hawks opened the end of January. She has amazing cinnamon rolls, donuts, cookies, paninis, salads, soups, and the best specialty coffees in the county. She is also an author, fabric designer, quilter, wife and mother. Pretty amazing if you ask me.

4-patch & snowball

QUILT SIZE
77½" X 95½"

DESIGNED BY
Jenny Doan

PIECED BY
Jenny Doan

QUILTED BY
Daniela Kirk

QUILT TOP
1 package 10" squares
3 yards solid – includes inner
   border

OUTER BORDER
1½ yards

BINDING
¾ yard

BACKING
7¼ yards

SAMPLE QUILT
Sewing Studio by Cynthia Frenette
for Robert Kaufman

ONLINE TUTORIALS
msqc.co/blockwinter16

QUILTING
Square Meander

PATTERN
pg. 24

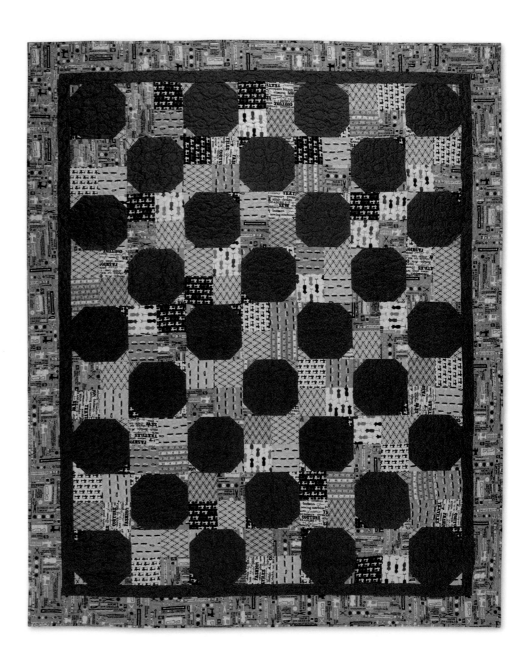

double square star

QUILT SIZE
62" X 75"

DESIGNED BY
Jenny Doan

PIECED BY
Carol Henderson

QUILTED BY
Sarah Richardson

QUILT TOP
3 packages 5" squares of the
    same fabric line
1¾ yards background

OUTER BORDER
1¼ yards

BINDING
¾ yard

BACKING
4 yards

SAMPLE QUILT
Botanique by Lila Tueller for Riley
Blake

ONLINE TUTORIALS
msqc.co/blockwinter16

QUILTING
Meandering Flowers

PATTERN
pg. 48

floating squares

QUILT SIZE
45½" X 54½"

DESIGNED BY
Jenny Doan

PIECED BY
Kelly McKenzie

QUILTED BY
Karen Russell

QUILT TOP
1 package 5" squares
2 yards background fabric (includes
   border)

BINDING
½ yard

BACKING
3 yards

SAMPLE QUILT
Pacific Warm by Elizabeth Hartman
for Robert Kaufman

ONLINE TUTORIALS
msqc.co/blockwinter16

QUILTING
Square Meander

PATTERN
pg. 32

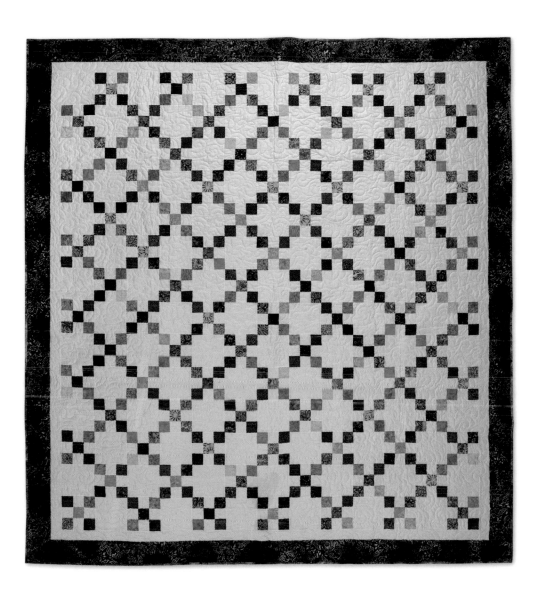

irish
chain

QUILT SIZE
91" X 97"

DESIGNED BY
Jenny Doan

PIECED BY
Jenny Doan

QUILTED BY
Kara Snow

QUILT TOP
1 roll of 2½" strips
5½ yards background – includes
    inner border

OUTER BORDER
1½ yards

BINDING
¾ yard

BACKING
8¼ yards

SAMPLE QUILT
Primo Batiks Radiant Reflections
by Marcus Fabrics

ONLINE TUTORIALS
msqc.co/blockwinter16

QUILTING
Free Swirls

PATTERN
pg. 8

lotus

QUILT SIZE
67" X 76½"

DESIGNED BY
Jenny Doan

PIECED BY
Carol Henderson

QUILTED BY
Karen Russell

QUILT TOP
1 package (42 ct.) 10" print squares
1 package (42 ct.) 10" background
   squares

BORDER
1¼ yards

BINDING
¾ yard

BACKING
4¾ yards

ADDITIONAL SUPPLIES
Large MSQC orange peel template
7¼ yards Heat N Bond Feather Lite
   Fusible Interfacing

SAMPLE QUILT
Into the Deep by Patty Sloniger for
Michael Miller

ONLINE TUTORIALS
msqc.co/blockwinter16

QUILTING
Flower Swirls

PATTERN
pg. 40

new flying geese

QUILT SIZE
54" X 63"

DESIGNED BY
Jenny Doan

PIECED BY
Carol Henderson

QUILTED BY
Sandi Gaunce

QUILT TOP
1 package (42 ct.) 10" squares
4 packages (42 ct.) white 5"
    squares background *or* 3 yards
    cut into 5" squares

BINDING
½ yard

BACKING
3½ yards

SAMPLE QUILT
Sunprints by Allison Glass for
Andover

ONLINE TUTORIALS
msqc.co/blockwinter16

QUILTING
Loops & Swirls

QUILT PATTERN
pg. 72

pinwheel party

QUILT SIZE
58½" X 63¾"

DESIGNED BY
Jenny Doan

PIECED BY
Cindy Morris

QUILTED BY
Sherry Melton

QUILT TOP
1 package 5" print squares (42 ct.)
2 yards background – includes
    inner border
⅓ yard solid or contrasting color
    for flange

OUTER BORDER
1¼ yards

BINDING
¾ yard

BACKING
3¾ yards

SAMPLE QUILT
Aria by Kate Spain for Moda

ONLINE TUTORIALS
msqc.co/blockwinter16

QUILTING
Forget Me Not

QUILT PATTERN
pg. 16

prairie flower

QUILT SIZE
74" X 89½"

DESIGNED BY
Jenny Doan

PIECED BY
Carol Henderson

QUILTED BY
Linda Frump

QUILT TOP
1 package 10" squares
3½ yards background fabric
 (includes sashing and inner
 border)
¼ yard for cornerstones

OUTER BORDER
1½ yards

BINDING
¾ yard

BACKING
5½ yards

SAMPLE QUILT
Lulabelle by Dodi Lee Poulsen for
Riley Blake

ONLINE TUTORIALS
msqc.co/blockwinter16

QUILTING
Botanical Blossoms

PATTERN
pg. 56

ribbon
star

QUILT SIZE
68″ X 82″

DESIGNED BY
Jenny Doan

PIECED BY
Cindy Morris

QUILTED BY
James Evenson

QUILT TOP
1 roll of 2½″ print strips
1 roll of 2½″ white strips (42 ct.)
   or 3 yards background fabric

OUTER BORDER
1½ yards

BINDING
¾ yard

BACKING
5 yards

SAMPLE QUILT
Dreamweaver by Amy Butler for
Free Spirit

ONLINE TUTORIALS
msqc.co/blockwinter16

QUILTING
Champagne Bubbles

PATTERN
pg. 80

studio
star

QUILT SIZE
58" X 74"

DESIGNED BY
Jenny Doan

PIECED BY
Kelly McKenzie

QUILTED BY
 Mari Zullig

QUILT TOP
1 roll 2½" print strips
3¼ yards background fabric –
   includes inner border

OUTER BORDER
1 yard

BINDING
¾ yard

BACKING
5 yards

SAMPLE QUILT
Black Tie Affair by BasicGrey for
Moda

ONLINE TUTORIALS
msqc.co/blockwinter16

QUILTING
Loops & Swirls

PATTERN
pg. 64

construction basics

- All seams are ¼" inch unless directions specify differently.

- Cutting instructions are given at the point when cutting is required.

- Precuts are not prewashed; therefore do not prewash other fabrics in the project

- All strips are cut WOF

- Remove all selvages

- All yardages based on 42" WOF

ACRONYMS USED

MSQC	Missouri Star Quilt Co.
RST	right sides together
WST	wrong sides together
HST	half-square triangle
WOF	width of fabric
LOF	length of fabric

pre-cut glossary

5" SQUARE PACK
1 = (42) 5" squares or ¾ yd of fabric
1 = baby
2 = crib
3 = lap
4 = twin

2½" STRIP ROLL
1 = (40) 2½" strip roll cut the width of fabric
    or 2¾ yds of fabric
1 = a twin
2 = queen

10" SQUARE PACK
1 = (42) 10" square pack of fabric: 2¾ yds total
1 = a twin
2 = queen

When we mention a precut, we are basing the pattern on a 40-42 count pack. Not all precuts have the same count, so be sure to check the count on your precut to make sure you have enough pieces to complete your project.

general quilting
- All seams are ¼" inch unless directions specify differently.
- Cutting instructions are given at the point when cutting is required.
- Precuts are not prewashed; therefore do not prewash other fabrics in the project.
- All strips are cut width of fabric.
- Remove all selvages.
- All yardages based on 42" width of fabric (WOF).

press seams
- Use the cotton setting on your iron when pressing.
- Press the seam just as it was sewn RST. This "sets" the seam.
- To set the seam, press just as it was sewn with right sides together.
- With dark fabric on top, lift the dark fabric and press back.
- The seam allowance is pressed toward the dark side. Some patterns may direct otherwise for certain situations.
- Press toward borders. Pieced borders may demand otherwise.
- Press diagonal seams open on binding to reduce bulk.

borders
- Always measure the quilt top 3 times before cutting borders.
- Start measuring about 4" in from each side and through the center vertically.
- Take the average of those 3 measurements.
- Cut 2 border strips to that size. Piece strips together if needed.
- Attach one to either side of the quilt.
- Position the border fabric on top as you sew. The feed dogs can act like rufflers. Having the border on top will prevent waviness and keep the quilt straight.
- Repeat this process for the top and bottom borders, measuring the width 3 times.
- Include the newly attached side borders in your measurements.
- Press toward the borders.

binding

find a video tutorial at: www.msqc.co/006

- Use 2½" strips for binding.
- Sew strips end-to-end into one long strip with diagonal seams, aka plus sign method (next). Press seams open.
- Fold in half lengthwise wrong sides together and press.
- The entire length should equal the outside dimension of the quilt plus 15" - 20."

plus sign method

- Lay one strip across the other as if to make a plus sign right sides together.
- Sew from top inside to bottom outside corners crossing the intersections of fabric as you sew. Trim excess to ¼" seam allowance.
- Press seam open.

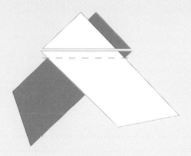

attach binding

- Match raw edges of folded binding to the quilt top edge.
- Leave a 10" tail at the beginning.
- Use a ¼" seam allowance.
- Start in the middle of a long straight side.

find a video tutorial at: www.msqc.co/001

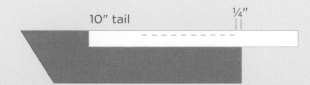

10" tail   ¼"

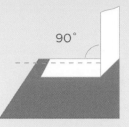
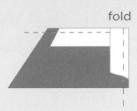

90°   fold

miter corners

- Stop sewing ¼" before the corner.
- Move the quilt out from under the presser foot.
- Clip the threads.
- Flip the binding up at a 90˚ angle to the edge just sewn.
- Fold the binding down along the next side to be sewn, aligning raw edges.
- The fold will lie along the edge just completed.
- Begin sewing on the fold.

close binding

*MSQC recommends **The Binding Tool** from TQM Products to finish binding perfectly every time.*

- Stop sewing when you have 12" left to reach the start.
- Where the binding tails come together, trim excess leaving only 2½" of overlap.
- It helps to pin or clip the quilt together at the two points where the binding starts and stops. This takes the pressure off of the binding tails while you work.
- Use the plus sign method to sew the two binding ends together, except this time when making the plus sign, match the edges. Using a pencil, mark your sewing line because you won't be able to see where the corners intersect. Sew across.

plus sign with matched edges

- Trim off excess; press seam open.
- Fold in half wrong sides together, and align all raw edges to the quilt top.
- Sew this last binding section to the quilt. Press.
- Turn the folded edge of the binding around to the back of the quilt and tack into place with an invisible stitch or machine stitch if you wish.

HIDEAWAY IN QUILT TOWN, USA

PART 6

Warehouse Rescue

—— *A JENNY DOAN MYSTERY* ——

written by Steve Westover

The end of Jin's final workday came quickly. She logged off her computer for the last time and stared at the MSQC logo bouncing around the screen. Her co-workers gathered their belongings and filed down the stairs to the exit. Only Sean remained. He stood in front of the observation window with his arms folded as he watched workers empty from the warehouse. He tapped his iPad control and the lights in the warehouse started to dim.

"Good night," Jin said as she stood and pushed in her chair. "Thank you for allowing me to work with you. It's been a pleasure."

Sean turned in place. His mouth opened to speak but nothing came out. A strange combination of relief and disappointment reflected in his eyes as his shoulders hunched. Jin didn't know what else to say so she nodded and left. Outside she climbed into one of the tandem seats on Jenny's tricycle and began her ride back to the main shop. The tires slipped and crunched the gravel beneath her but her mind didn't register the sound. Hamilton and MSQC had been good to her but she concentrated on where she could go next, realizing she hadn't developed a Plan B.

Jin rode down Main Street and pulled the trike onto the sidewalk in front of the shop, oblivious to the dark Mercedes van parked a block away near JC Penney's boyhood home.

At the Blue Sage Jenny paid Jin for her work with a handful of cash while they waited for their food. Jenny tried to engage in conversation but Jin's focus was elsewhere. She wasn't being rude, just distracted. And she looked like she aged ten years over the course of the day. "I'm really sorry, Jin. Will you be sticking around town for a while?"

Jin shook her head listlessly.

"Where will you go? Home? Maybe things are cleared up and it would be safe," Jenny suggested. Again, Jin shook her head. The meal and one-sided conversation seemed to last hours. Finally Jenny asked, "Would you like me to take you somewhere? Do you need any ...?"

Jin began to shake her head again but then her eyes widened. "Oh." The one syllable word stretched for a mile. "I can't believe I did that," Jin muttered after a joyless chuckle.

"What?"

Jin swallowed the last sip of her soda. "It's nothing. Just a book I

was reading. Two chapters left. I think I left it in the break room but no big deal."

"Well, maybe not, but we can drive over to pick it up. I hate it when I don't get closure from a good book. I'll text Sean to have him unlock the door remotely and turn on the lights. Let's go."

Jenny pulled up to the main warehouse entrance unaware of the two well-dressed killers lurking in the dark van. As expected the warehouse door was unlocked when they arrived. "Grab your book and I'll be just a minute," Jenny said. "Sean will re-lock everything in five minutes so we'll need to be quick."

Jenny entered a small office on the main floor and closed the door while Jin went upstairs to retrieve her book. Jenny checked voicemail, scribbled notes, and then went to exit. She turned the knob and pulled on the door but it didn't budge. She took a step back and glared at the obstinate door. Once again the knob turned easily but the door wouldn't open. She pulled again. Nothing.

Pounding on the door with the side of her fist, Jenny called out. "Jin?" She listened for a response. "Jin. I think my door's stuck." She waited for Jin to answer but there was only silence. Jenny pounded again. Nothing. Jenny rolled a chair beside the vexing door and continued to pound intermittently. Between knocking she texted Sean and then leaned back in her chair, resigned to wait. Her phone display read- Text Rejected. She tapped the screen to resend. "What's going on?" she muttered and then pounded on the door again. "JIN!" She stared at her phone but once again, in bright red- Text Rejected.

Jenny began dialing Sean's number when the crash of two gunshots reverberated from behind the closed door. "JIN," she screamed. Then she turned the handle and pulled with all of her might. No movement. Then another shot echoed. Jenny's heart raced as she pounded the door. "JIN!"

Rushing to the desk, Jenny picked up the office phone to call for help but was met by dead silence. In a near panic for Jin's safety, as well as her own, she frantically searched the desk drawers for a tool to aid her escape. Then two ideas hit her at once. She abandoned the drawer and stood upright, squared her shoulders, and inhaled a calming breath. "Please work," she muttered as she implemented idea #1.

She pulled her smart phone from her pocket and stared at the display. The Wi-Fi signal was strong. The intruders had disabled the phone and even her 4G cellular reception, but they hadn't thought to block the Wi-Fi network. Jenny felt hope swelling inside her as she opened her Facebook AP. She simultaneously messaged Sean, her husband, and MK to send police but there was no immediate response. "Please work," she repeated and then crammed the phone into her pocket.

Though hopeful for a quick emergency response Jenny knew she couldn't rely on it. Jin needed help NOW. Jenny moved to idea #2; her escape from the office. Beside the desk sat a fire extinguisher that had yet to be mounted on the wall. She picked it up and then pressed her ear to the door and listened, hoping the intruders were far away. She lifted the fire extinguisher and slammed it onto the doorknob. The knob wobbled and she hit it repeatedly until it fell to the floor with a clank. With a letter opener from the desk she pried out the locking mechanism from inside the door and then stuck her fingers into the hole where the knob had been. She pulled. It still wouldn't open. Jenny felt her hopes deflating when she had idea #3. With the letter opener she pried the pin out of the door's middle hinge, and then the bottom. After struggling with the last hinge at the top the pin finally fell to the floor.

With the pins removed Jenny hoped and prayed the door would open. She jammed her fingers back into the knob hole and pulled. She felt a slight shift from where the hinges had been so she applied pressure while reaching with her other hand to pull the middle hinge. She took a deep breath and then pulled. She felt movement so she pulled harder until the door slipped off the hinge. With the weight of the door threatening to fall on top of her, Jenny pushed it to her right while she lurched to the left. The door crashed into the room.

Peeking her head outside the office, Jenny glanced first to the left into the shipping area and then toward the warehouse and an exit to the right. She instantly thought of dashing for freedom but stopped as she heard the shuffle of feet and a growly male whisper coming toward her. The sounds drew closer and Jenny knew she had to make a decision; stay or go; save herself or help Jin. Jenny only thought for a split second and then hurried away from the approaching intruder and past the exit toward the warehouse. She scurried around a corner and pressed her back against the wall.

"What am I doing?" Jenny moaned quietly as she felt exposed in the brightly lit warehouse. She entertained doubts about the wisdom of her choice. She sidestepped quietly along the wall and surveyed the tall metal shelves filled with product. She paused mid-step as her phone vibrated inside her pocket. She fumbled and then read her Facebook notification.

MOM-WHAT'S HAPPENING? Sean screamed through the message.

Jenny began typing her response when she noticed movement and a hissing sound coming from a low shelf across a wide aisle. She heard it again. "Pssssssst."

Jenny looked closely and saw her friend hiding behind two stacked pallets of BLOCK magazine. "Jin, are you okay?" Jenny mouthed.

Jin's lips were tight and her brow knit into one. With one finger she pointed upwards. Jenny looked up. Even with her back pressed against the wall Jenny could feel the shadowy presence of a large man standing at the observation window, watching. The image sent chills down her neck all the way to her toes.

Still holding the phone Jenny typed quickly in response to Sean's message. Cut the lights. Then, getting Jin's attention again, Jenny mouthed the words, "Get Ready."

Jenny listened to the deliberate footsteps of the second man walking towards the cavernous warehouse. She glanced toward the overhead lights and waited for what felt like a lifetime, her breathing matching every beat of her heart. Each second ticked away in slow motion, adding to the fear she would be discovered by the approaching intruder or seen by the watcher at the window. She listened closely to the footsteps and then the silence when they paused. Then the lights made a soft click before dimming.

"Now!" Jenny screamed with a whisper as she ran across the aisle to Jin's hiding place. Grabbing Jin's hand Jenny pulled her out from behind a crate as she ran between rows of shelves. Glancing back Jenny could no longer see the intruder watching from the now blackened window.

"Where are we going?" Jin asked, her voice shaking with fear.

"We'll get out through... the delivery bay," Jenny said between heavy breaths. Then the explosion of another gunshot echoed through the warehouse. Shattered glass from the observation window cascaded to the concrete floor before another shot rang out and ricocheted with a metallic clang. "Stay low."

At the end of the long aisle Jin and Jenny took cover behind a crate as they caught their breath. Jenny pointed through the darkness toward the northeast corner of the building. "There. The button to raise the bay door is on the left. It will take a few seconds to rise. Are you ready?" Jenny rose up and leaned forward awkwardly with her hands pressed to the floor like a sprinter awaiting the starting pistol.

"No. Wait," Jin said. "I tried to get out of the main door. It t was locked. Will this work?"

Jenny thought for a moment. "There's one way to be sure." She messaged Sean over Facebook. *Unlock doors. Raise NE delivery bay.* She cupped her hand to block the light from the screen but held it out so both she and Jin could read Sean's response.

All doors unlocked. Can't raise door...

"Can't raise the door? What are we going to do?" Jin asked, sharing a worried look with Jenny.

Then the rest of Sean's message came through ... remotely. Jenny read the entire message in a whisper. "Can't raise door remotely." Jenny's considered options. "We can lift it ourselves but the door is too exposed."

"We need a diversion," Jin suggested.

"Exactly," Jenny agreed. "And I think I know just what to do. Get ready to go for the door. Pull the latch at the bottom on the far left and lift."

"What are you going to do?"

Jenny didn't have time to answer. "Are you ready?" Jenny asked. Jin nodded. "Go now." Jenny watched Jin cling to the crate. "Jin, trust me. You need to go now. I'll take care of the rest." Jenny felt Jin's fear. Then she quietly commanded, "Now."

Jin took off running toward the northeast bay door 20 yards to her right as Jenny scrambled to her left. Picking up one of the unusual skateboards with the joint in the middle, Jenny climbed onto the orange Hyster forklift. She turned the key and pressed a button. The forklift hummed to life. Cranking the wheel to her left she stepped on the gas and then pulled a lever on the dash, raising the forks. Turning down an aisle the explosion of a gunshot and the metallic ricochet of a bullet off the front fork caused her to instinctively drop to the floor. With one hand on the gas pedal she pressed one end of the skateboard against the pedal and wedged the other end against the seat.

"Sean's going to kill me," she muttered. Another shot ricocheted even closer so she slid out of the forklift and onto the concrete floor. Her knee banged first and then her wrist before the rest of her body hit. Jenny looked up from the ground as the forklift moved forward slowly. She heard another shot and another ricochet off the forklift. The diversion was working.

Despite the throbbing in her knee Jenny hobbled to the end of the dark aisle. Looking toward the bay she could see Jin's silhouette as the door raised 4 feet off the ground. Then Jin hunched down and rushed out. Jenny felt a mixture of relief, happiness and loneliness.

The crash of the forklift hitting the wall below the observation window punctuated the urgency Jenny felt. She listened to the racing steps and cursing sounds coming from the men who finally seemed to realize the forklift was a decoy. Jenny took a deep breath and then raced the eight feet across the aisle to a secure location near the next shelf. She waited a moment and then ran across another aisle but this time shots rang out. A burn cut across her forearm. Instead of stopping at the next aisle Jenny kept running, her eyes scanning the opening at the northeast bay.

"MOM!" Tears instantly flowed as Jenny heard Sean's voice and saw his silhouette slide into the warehouse. She heard him call. "Mom, hurry."

Jenny panted and winced in pain with every unsteady step. She heard the footsteps of her attackers nearby and imagined a flurry of bullets burning into her back. But Sean urged her on so she kept running toward him as he ran toward her. She listened for the sound of gunshots that would signal her impending death but she reached Sean without a single shot.

Sean stood behind his mother, pressing gently as he turned and raced with her toward the bay opening. Only feet from the bright opening the anticipated shot rang out. Jenny instinctively dove toward the bay door as Sean pushed her toward it. She hit the concrete floor and rolled through the opening into the blinding light. Blinded by the light she looked back expecting to see Sean rolling through the opening after her. Jenny's teeth clenched and her body shook when he didn't appear. Standing, Jenny hurried toward the opening but felt thick arms wrap around her and pull her away. She fought harder trying to get back to Sean inside the warehouse but a police officer held her tight. Cars slid to a stop in the gravel behind her with sirens blazing. Doors opened and slammed.

"Sean!" Jenny screamed as three Sheriff's Deputies sprinted toward the bay opening. "Sean's still in there," she yelled as the first Deputy crawled inside. Jenny wiped tears from her eyes as she hyperventilated. Then she saw Sean dragged out by one hand. As the officer helped him to his feet Jenny's knees went wobbly and she dropped to the ground, her body shaking from a combination of joy and shock. She blinked once, long and hard.

Jenny's eyes opened to the harshness of smelling salts as EMT's strapped her onto a gurney. She saw Sean sitting on a gurney of his own and Jin leaning against the Sheriff's SUV as she answered questions. The bay door was wide open and teams of police were streaming in and out. Then her eyes closed again.

***

Aside from a few bullet holes and a crude forklift-sized door in the warehouse wall Jenny took the worst of the abuse with a bruised knee, a knot on her forehead, a bullet graze across her right forearm and a sprained left wrist. After a restful weekend of observation at Cameron Regional she was released.

"You need to take it easy, Mom," Sean said. "You won't be doing any quilting for a while." He walked beside his dad who wheeled Jenny out of the front hospital entrance. Sean limped slightly from his own superficial gunshot wound on his lower leg. Sean was sure the girls would be impressed even if his mother wasn't.

"Is Jin still around or has she left yet?" Jenny asked.

"She left this morning," MK called out from behind. "She'll be back in her own bed by tonight. She seemed pretty excited about it."

"Is she safe returning home?" Jenny asked.

"Oh, sure," Sean said. Those two clowns from the warehouse spilled the beans and the police picked up some big-wig developer in Chicago. Apparently Jin's boss was hurting his business so he sent the goons to take care of it. Rumor is they made some kind of a deal."

"As long as Jin's okay, I'm happy for her," Jenny said.

"She asked me to give you something," MK said. The entourage stopped near the car and MK pulled out a plastic grocery sack and a handwritten card.

"What is it?" Jenny asked.

"Jin left you a note," MK said.

Jenny took a moment to read it and then dabbed the moisture from the corner of her eyes.

"And this?" MK added. "It's a table runner...I think," She removed a slender, quilted ... something. "Jin said it was her first attempt at quilting and she wanted you to have it. Something about you being her inspiration," MK said with a chuckle. "It's really pretty sweet. Hideous, but sweet."

Jenny laughed as she held Jin's parting gift. "Good for her. We'll make a quilter out of her yet."